T H E   B O O K   O F

FONDUES

THE BOOK OF
FONDUES

LORNA RHODES

Photography by
SIMON BUTCHER

HPBooks

ANOTHER BEST-SELLING VOLUME FROM HPBOOKS

HP Books
Published by The Berkley Publishing Group
A division of Penguin Putnam Inc.
375 Hudson Street
New York, New York 10014

22

The Penguin Putnam Inc. World Wide Web site address is
http://www.penguinputnam.com

Library of Congress Cataloging-in-Publication Data

Rhodes, Lorna.
  The book of fondues

  Includes index.
  1. Fondue.   I. Title
TX85.R47 1988   641.8   87-15052
ISBN 0-89586-667-6

Printed and bound in Spain

CONTENTS

INTRODUCTION

A fondue party is a really enjoyable way to entertain informally. The preparation is done in advance so that the hostess can relax with her guests, dipping tasty morsels. *The Book of Fondues* contains over a hundred recipes for savory and sweet fondues with a truly international flavor, plus lots of ideas for food to dip and accompaniments.

There are many types of fondue sets on the market. Each contains a pot, a stand on which the pot rests and a burner for cooking or keeping the food hot at the table. The enameled cast-iron or metal pots are suitable for deep-fried fondues, but if used for cheese or dessert fondues the heat should be kept low. The earthenware or pottery fondue pots resemble the original Swiss *caquelon* used for cheese fondues. It is well shaped for swirling foods in cheese, but do not attempt to use them for deep-fried fondues. The small fondue pots are used for desserts and the candle burner is adequate to keep the sauce warm. In addition to the fondue set you will need long forks or bamboo skewers to spear the food.

FONDUE EQUIPMENT

The word fondue comes from the French word *fondre*, meaning to melt. The traditional Swiss fondue is a delicious mixture of melted Emmentaler and Gruyère cheeses and wine. In this book a wide variety of cheeses are used to create cheese fondue recipes from around the world.

Once the cheese fondue is cooked it is placed over the burner at the table. From then on it must be constantly stirred to prevent burning. This can be done as the guests dip in bread, vegetables and cubes of cold meat. A crust will form on the bottom of the pot which can be scraped out and divided between the guests at the end.

Other popular fondues use hot vegetable oil to cook the food. Fill the pot a third full with vegetable oil and heat on the stove until it reaches 375F (190C); then carefully transfer the pot to the burner on the table. If too much food is added to the oil the temperature will drop, so reheating on the stove will be necessary. At the table each person spears a piece of meat, fish or vegetable with a fondue

fork and places it in the oil until cooked to their taste. You may want to have a plate lined with paper towels available to drain the food on before eating, especially when serving crumbly or batter-dipped fondues. All these fondues are served with a variety of sauces, and there are many recipes for accompaniments from which to choose.

The fondue pot is an extremely versatile piece of equipment and lends itself to such dishes as Mongolian Hotpot, which uses simmering chicken broth to cook the food. As the food cooks the broth becomes more flavorful and is served as a soup at the end of the meal.

The Book of Fondues also contains recipes for vegetarian dips and an exciting choice of sweet fondues. Illustrated throughout with attractive color photographs, here is a wonderful collection of recipes and ideas for fondue cooking and entertaining.

Classic Swiss Fondue

1 garlic clove, halved
1 cup dry white wine
1 teaspoon lemon juice
2 cups (8 oz.) shredded Gruyère cheese
2 cups (8 oz.) shredded Emmentaler cheese
2 teaspoons cornstarch
2 tablespoons kirsch
Dash white pepper
Pinch grated nutmeg

To Serve:
French bread, cut in cubes

Rub inside of fondue pot with cut garlic clove.

Pour in wine and lemon juice; cook over medium heat until bubbly. Turn heat to low and gradually stir in cheeses with a wooden spoon.

In a small bowl blend cornstarch with kirsch. Blend into cheese and continue to cook, stirring, 2 to 3 minutes or until mixture is thick and smooth. Do not allow fondue to boil. Season with white pepper and nutmeg. Serve with bread cubes. Makes about 4 servings.

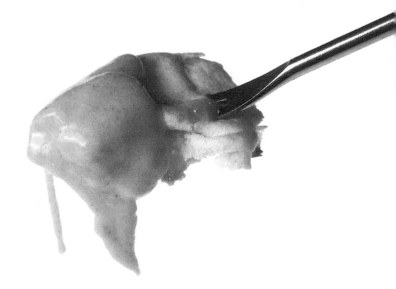

Curried Cheese Fondue

1 garlic clove, halved
2/3 cup dry white wine
1 teaspoon lemon juice
2 teaspoons curry paste
8 oz. process Gruyère cheese
8 oz. Cheddar cheese
1 teaspoon cornstarch
2 tablespoons dry sherry

To Serve:
pita bread rounds, cut in pieces

Shred cheeses.

Rub inside of fondue pot with cut garlic clove. Pour in wine and lemon juice; cook over medium heat until bubbly. Turn heat to low and add curry paste. Gradually stir in shredded cheeses.

In a small bowl blend cornstarch with sherry. Blend into cheese and continue to cook, stirring, 2 to 3 minutes or until mixture is thick and smooth. Do not allow fondue to boil. Serve with pieces of pita bread rounds. Makes 4 to 6 servings.

Somerset Fondue

1 small onion, halved
1 cup apple cider
1 teaspoon lemon juice
3 cups (12 oz.) shredded Cheddar cheese
1/2 teaspoon dry mustard
1 tablespoon cornstarch
3 tablespoons apple juice
Dash white pepper

To Serve:
wedges of apple, cubes of bread

Rub inside of fondue pot with cut side of onion.

Pour in cider and lemon juice; cook over medium heat until bubbly. Turn heat to low and gradually stir in cheese. Continue to heat until cheese melts.

In a small bowl blend mustard and cornstarch with apple juice. Blend into cheese and continue to cook, stirring, 2 to 3 minutes or until mixture is thick and creamy. Season with white pepper. Serve with apple wedges and cubes of crusty bread. Makes about 6 servings.

Smoky German Fondue

1 small onion, halved
1 cup light ale
3 cups (12 oz.) shredded smoky cheese
1 cup (4 oz.) shredded Emmentaler cheese
1 tablespoon cornstarch
3 tablespoons milk
1 teaspoon German-style mustard

To Serve:
rye bread, cooked frankfurters

Measure ingredients. Rub inside of fondue pot
with cut side of onion.

Pour ale in fondue pot and warm over medium
heat until bubbly. Turn heat to low and gradually stir in cheeses. Continue to heat until cheese
melts.

In a small bowl blend cornstarch with milk.
Blend into cheese, add mustard and continue to
cook, stirring, 2 to 3 minutes or until mixture is
thick and creamy. Serve with cubes of rye bread
and pieces of cooked frankfurters. Makes 4 to 6
servings.

Blue-Cheese Fondue

1 cup milk
1 (8-oz.) pkg. cream cheese, room temperature
2 cups (8 oz.) crumbled blue cheese
1/2 teaspoon garlic salt
1 tablespoon cornstarch
2 tablespoons half and half

To Serve:
cubes of ham or sausage and crusty bread

Put milk and cream cheese in fondue pot and beat with an electric mixer until creamy and smooth.

Place fondue pot over low heat and gradually stir in blue cheese. Continue to stir over heat until smooth.

In a small bowl blend garlic salt and cornstarch with half and half. Blend into cheese and cook, stirring, 2 to 3 minutes longer or until thick and creamy. Serve with cubes of ham or sausage and cubes of crusty bread. Makes 4 to 6 servings.

—————— Cheese & Onion Fondue ——————

2 tablespoons butter
1 large onion, chopped
2 teaspoons all-purpose flour
2/3 cup sour cream
2 cups (8 oz.) shredded Gruyère cheese
2 cups (8 oz.) shredded Cheddar cheese
2 tablespoons snipped chives
Pepper

To Serve:
small cooked potatoes and sausages

Melt butter in a large saucepan, add onion and cook 4 to 5 minutes or until soft but not brown.

Stir in flour; add sour cream and cook 2 minutes. Add cheeses and continue to cook, stirring, until mixture is smooth.

Add chives and season with pepper. Pour into fondue pot and serve with small cooked potatoes and sausages. Makes 4 to 6 servings.

Italian Fondue

1 garlic clove, halved
1-1/4 cups milk
2 cups (8 oz.) shredded mozzarella cheese
8 oz. blue cheese, cubed
1/2 cup (1-1/2 oz.) finely grated Parmesan
  cheese
2 teaspoons cornstarch
3 tablespoons dry white wine

To Serve:
salami, bread sticks and olives

Rub inside of fondue pot with cut garlic clove.
Add milk and heat until bubbly

Stir in all cheeses and continue to heat until
melted.

Blend cornstarch with wine, blend into cheese
mixture and cook, stirring, 2 to 3 minutes or
until thick and creamy. Serve with slices of
rolled-up salami or a stick of salami cut in
cubes, bread sticks and olives. Makes 4 to 6
servings.

Dutch Fondue

1 small onion, halved
1 cup milk
4 cups (1 lb.) shredded Gouda cheese
2 teaspoons caraway seeds
1 tablespoon cornstarch
3 tablespoons gin
Pepper

To Serve:
mushrooms, cubes of light rye bread

Measure ingredients. Rub inside of fondue pot with cut side of onion.

Add milk and heat until bubbly; then gradually stir in cheese. Continue to heat until cheese melts.

Stir in caraway seeds. In a small bowl blend cornstarch with gin. Blend into cheese mixture and cook, stirring, 2 to 3 minutes or until smooth and creamy. Season with pepper. Serve with mushrooms and light rye bread. Makes 4 to 6 servings.

Pub Fondue

1 garlic clove, halved
1-1/4 cups beer
2 cups (8 oz.) shredded Leicester or mild
   Cheddar cheese
2 cups (8 oz.) shredded sharp Cheddar cheese
1 tablespoon all-purpose flour
1 teaspoon dry mustard
Pepper

To Serve:
cubes of whole-wheat bread, pickles

Rub inside of fondue pot with cut garlic clove. Add beer and heat until bubbly.

Toss cheeses in flour and mustard.

Over low heat add cheeses to beer. Season with pepper and continue to heat, stirring constantly, until mixture is smooth. Serve with whole-wheat bread cubes and pickles. Makes 4 to 6 servings.

Rosé Fondue

1 garlic clove, halved
1 cup rosé wine
1 cup (4 oz.) shredded Gruyère cheese
2 cups (8 oz.) shredded Cheddar cheese with
   wine
1 tablespoon cornstarch
2 tablespoons kirsch

To Serve:
French bread, cut in cubes

Rub inside of fondue pot with cut garlic clove.
Add wine and heat until bubbly.

Gradually stir in cheeses and continue to cook
over medium heat until melted.

In a small bowl mix cornstarch with kirsch;
blend into cheese mixture. Cook, stirring, 2 to 3
minutes or until smooth and thickened. Serve
with cubes of French bread. Makes about 6
servings.

Beer Fondue

1 tablespoon butter
1 small onion, chopped
1 cup light ale
4 cups (1 lb.) shredded Lancashire or Monterey
   Jack cheese
4 teaspoons cornstarch
5 tablespoons half and half

To Serve:
cauliflower florets, radishes and mushrooms

Melt butter in a large saucepan and cook onion until soft. Pour in ale and heat until bubbly.

Over low heat, stir in cheese. Continue to heat until cheese has melted.

In a small bowl blend cornstarch with half and half. Add to cheese mixture and cook, stirring, 2 to 3 minutes or until smooth and thickened. Serve with cauliflower florets, radishes and mushrooms. Makes 4 to 6 servings.

Danish Fondue

9 slices (6 oz.) finely chopped lean bacon
1 small onion, chopped
1 tablespoon butter
1 tablespoon all-purpose flour
1 cup beer
2 cups (8 oz.) shredded Havarti cheese
2 cups (8 oz.) shredded Samsø cheese

To Serve:
small sweet and sour gherkins, light rye bread

Put bacon, onion and butter in a large saucepan and cook until bacon is golden and onion is soft.

Stir in flour. Gradually add beer and cook until thickened.

Add cheeses and cook, stirring constantly, until melted and the mixture is smooth. Pour into fondue pot and serve with gherkins and cubes of light rye bread. Makes 4 to 6 servings.

Israeli Fondue

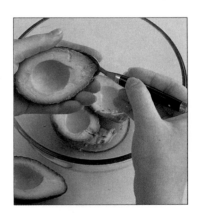

2 medium-size avocados, halved
1 tablespoon lemon juice
1 garlic clove, halved
3/4 cup dry white wine
3 cups (12 oz.) shredded Edam cheese
2 teaspoons cornstarch
1/3 cup sour cream

To Serve:
French bread, red and green bell peppers and cured dried beef (bresaola)

Scoop flesh from avocados into a bowl and mash with lemon juice until smooth.

Rub inside of fondue pot with cut garlic clove. Pour in wine and heat until bubbly. Over low heat, stir in cheese and cook until melted.

In a small bowl blend cornstarch and sour cream. Add this and the mashed avocados to the cheese mixture. Continue to cook, stirring, 4 to 5 minutes or until thick and smooth. Serve with cubes of French bread; bell peppers, cut in strips; and bresaola. Makes about 6 servings.

Normandy Fondue

1 garlic clove, halved
1/2 cup dry white wine
2/3 cup half and half
12 oz. Camembert cheese, rind removed
1 tablespoon cornstarch
1/4 cup calvados brandy

To Serve:
French bread, chunks of apple

Rub inside of fondue pot with cut garlic clove.
Add wine and half and half; heat until bubbly.

Cut cheese in small pieces and add to wine
mixture. Stir over low heat until melted.

In a small bowl blend cornstarch with calvados;
add to cheese mixture. Continue to cook, stirring 2 to 3 minutes or until thick and creamy.
Serve with cubes of French bread and chunks of
apple. Makes about 6 servings.

Highland Fondue

1 small onion, chopped
1 tablespoon butter
1 cup milk
4 cups (1 lb.) shredded Cheddar cheese
1 tablespoon cornstarch
1/4 cup whisky

To Serve:
cubes of rye and onion breads

In a medium-size saucepan cook onion in butter over low heat until soft. Add milk and heat until bubbly.

Gradually stir in cheese and continue to cook until melted.

In a small bowl blend cornstarch with whisky; stir into cheese mixture. Cook, stirring, 2 to 3 minutes or until thickened. Pour into fondue pot and serve with cubes of rye and onion breads. Makes 4 to 6 servings.

Welsh Fondue

2 tablespoons butter
1/2 lb. leeks, trimmed and finely chopped
2 tablespoons all-purpose flour
1 cup beer
2-1/2 cups (10 oz.) shredded Caerphilly cheese
Pepper

To Serve:
cubes of French bread

In a large saucepan melt butter over low heat. Add leeks, cover pan and cook 10 minutes or until tender.

Stir in flour and cook 1 minute. Add beer and heat, stirring constantly, until thickened.

Gradually add cheese and continue to cook, stirring, until cheese melts. Season with pepper. Pour into fondue pot and serve with cubes of French bread. Makes 4 to 6 servings.

Celebration Fondue

1 garlic clove, halved
1 cup champagne
1 cup (4 oz.) shredded Emmentaler cheese
3 cups (12 oz.) shredded Port du Salut cheese
2 egg yolks
1/4 cup half and half
2 teaspoons cornstarch
2 tablespoons brandy

To Serve:
rolls of ham and cubes of French bread

Rub inside of fondue pot with cut side of garlic clove. Add champagne and heat until bubbly.

Gradually add cheeses. As cheeses begin to melt beat in egg yolks and half and half.

In a small bowl blend cornstarch and brandy; stir into cheese mixture. Continue to cook, stirring constantly, until thick and creamy. Serve with rolls of ham and cubes of French bread. Makes 4 to 6 servings.

Deviled Cheese Fondue

1 garlic clove, halved
3/4 cup milk
3 cups (12 oz.) shredded smoky Cheddar cheese
2 tablespoons all-purpose flour
2 teaspoons Worcestershire sauce
2 teaspoons prepared horseradish
1 teaspoon prepared mustard

To Serve:
cubes of ham, cubes of toasted whole-wheat bread

Rub inside of fondue pot with cut garlic clove.
Add milk and heat until bubbly.

Toss cheese in flour; add to milk, Stir constantly
over low heat until cheese melts and mixture is
thick and smooth.

Stir in Worcestershire sauce, horseradish and
mustard. Serve with cubes of ham and toasted
whole-wheat bread. Makes about 6 servings.

Fondue Bourguignonne

2 lbs. beef tenderloin

Tomato Sauce:
1 tablespoon vegetable oil
2 shallots, finely chopped
1 garlic clove, crushed
1 (14-oz.) can crushed tomatoes
2 tablespoons tomato paste
Salt and pepper
1 tablespoon chopped parsley

To make Tomato Sauce, heat oil in a medium-size saucepan, add shallots and cook slowly until soft.

Stir in garlic, tomatoes with their juice and tomato paste. Season with salt and pepper then bring to a boil. Reduce heat and simmer uncovered about 30 minutes or until sauce has thickened. Stir in parsley and serve hot or cold.

Cut beef tenderloin in 1-inch cubes and place in a serving dish. Each person spears a cube of meat with a fondue fork and puts the meat in the hot oil to deep-fry. The meat cube is cooked according to the individual's taste. Makes about 4 to 6 servings.

Serve Creamy Horseradish Sauce, page 40, Garlic Sauce, page 55, Curry Sauce, page 31, and Mustard Sauce, page 41, also.

Bacon Bundles

12 slices (8 oz.) bacon
8 oz. chicken livers

Deviled Sauce:
1 tablespoon butter
1 shallot
1 tablespoon all-purpose flour
2/3 cup chicken broth
4 medium-size tomatoes, skinned, chopped
1 tablespoon tomato paste
2 teaspoons sugar
1 tablespoon red-wine vinegar
1 tablespoon Worcestershire sauce
1/2 teaspoon paprika
Dash cayenne pepper

Cut bacon slices in half. Trim chicken livers and cut in bite-size pieces.

Wrap bacon around chicken livers and spear on bamboo skewers; place on a serving plate.

To make Deviled Sauce, melt butter in a medium-size saucepan, add shallot and cook until soft. Stir in flour, then add remaining ingredients. Simmer 15 minutes; strain through a sieve. Serve hot. Makes about 4 servings.

Serve Creamy Onion Sauce, page 53, also.

Veal Milanese

1-1/2 lbs. cubed veal loin, leg or fillet
6 tablespoons all-purpose flour seasoned with
   salt and pepper
3 eggs, lightly beaten
2 teaspoons finely grated lemon peel
1-1/2 cups dry bread crumbs

Italian Sauce:
2 tablespoons olive oil
1 medium-size onion, finely chopped
1 to 2 garlic cloves, crushed
1-1/2 lbs. tomatoes, skinned, chopped
5 tablespoons dry white wine
1 tablespoon chopped fresh basil

Toss veal in seasoned flour, dip in beaten egg and coat in mixture of bread crumbs and lemon peel. Place on a serving plate.

To make Italian Sauce, heat oil in a medium-size saucepan. Add onion and garlic and cook over low heat until soft. Add tomatoes and wine. Season with salt and pepper; simmer 30 minutes.

Process sauce in a blender or food processor until smooth, or press through a sieve. Stir in basil and reheat sauce before serving. Makes 4 to 6 servings.

Serve also Lemon-Parsley Sauce, page 45, substituting chicken broth for fish stock.

Spicy Chicken Fondue

6 chicken breasts, boned, skinned
1/4 cup vegetable oil
2 teaspoons paprika
1/2 teaspoon chili powder

Curry Sauce:
1 medium-size onion, chopped
2 teaspoons curry powder
1 tablespoon all-purpose flour
1-1/4 cups milk
2 tablespoons mango chutney

Cut chicken in 3/4-inch pieces. Mix oil, paprika and chili powder together; stir in chicken.

To make Curry Sauce, heat 1 tablespoon vegetable oil in small saucepan, add onion and cook until soft. Stir in curry powder and cook 2 minutes; blend in flour.

Gradually stir in milk allowing mixture to slowly come to a boil. Continue cooking until sauce thickens. Simmer 5 minutes then add chutney and salt and pepper to taste. Serve hot. Makes 6 servings.

Serve Cucumber & Yogurt Sauce, page 41, also.

Fruity Duck Fondue

1-1/2 lbs. duck breast fillets
2 tablespoons all-purpose flour seasoned with
    salt, pepper and 1 teaspoon five spice powder

Marmalade Sauce:
1 tablespoon brown sugar
2/3 cup orange juice
1/4 cup orange marmalade
3 tablespoons lemon juice
1/4 cup raisins, chopped

Wine & Cherry Sauce:
1 tablespoon sugar
1 (16-oz.) can black cherries, drained, pitted
1/3 cup red wine
Pinch allspice

Cut duck in pieces 3/4 inch wide. Coat in sea-soned flour.

To make Marmalade Sauce, simmer brown sugar, orange juice, marmalade, lemon juice and raisins in a small saucepan 5 minutes.

To make Wine & Cherry Sauce, simmer sugar, cherries, wine and allspice in a small saucepan 15 minutes. Press through a sieve; serve sauce warm. Makes about 4 servings.

Serve Ginger Sauce, page 59, also.

Surprise Meatball Fondue

1-1/2 lbs. lean ground beef
1 tablespoon finely chopped onion
1/2 cup fresh whole-wheat bread crumbs
4 oz. Cheddar cheese, diced

Barbecue Sauce:
1 tablespoon tomato paste
1 tablespoon red-wine vinegar
2 tablespoons honey
2 teaspoons dry mustard
1 tablespoon Worcestershire sauce
1-1/4 cups chicken broth
2 teaspoons cornstarch
1/2 cup orange juice

In a bowl mix ground beef, onion and bread crumbs. Add salt and pepper to taste.

Shape meat mixture into 36 even-size balls. Flatten each ball slightly, place a piece of cheese in the middle and mold the meat around, sealing it well.

To make Barbecue Sauce, put tomato paste, vinegar, honey, dry mustard, Worcestershire sauce and broth in a small saucepan and simmer 10 minutes. Blend cornstarch with orange juice; stir into sauce and simmer 1 minute. Makes 4 to 6 servings.

Serve Mustard Sauce, page 41, and Chutney Sauce, page 35, also.

—————— Lamb Meatball Fondue ——————

1-1/4 lbs. ground lamb
3 green onions, finely chopped
1 cup fresh bread crumbs
2 tablespoons chopped parsley

Mushroom Sauce:
1/4 cup butter
1/3 lb. mushrooms, finely chopped
2 tablespoons flour
1-1/4 cups milk
1 tablespoon dry sherry

Mix together all ingredients for lamb meatballs. Season with salt and pepper to taste.

With wet hands shape mixture into walnut-size balls and place on a serving plate.

To make Mushroom Sauce, melt butter in a small saucepan, add mushrooms and sauté over low heat 5 minutes. Stir in flour then slowly add milk. Simmer for 5 minutes longer; add sherry. Serve warm. Makes about 6 servings.

Serve Hot Cranberry Dip, page 94, and Deviled Sauce, page 29, also.

Crispy Pork Bites

1 lb. very lean pork, finely ground
1 small onion, finely chopped
1/3 (8-oz.) pkg. cream cheese, room
  temperature
1 tablespoon chopped parsley
1 teaspoon prepared mustard
1/2 cup fresh bread crumbs
2 eggs, lightly beaten
3/4 cup dry bread crumbs

Chutney Sauce:
Tomato Sauce, page 28
2 tablespoons mango chutney

Put sausage and onion in a medium-size skillet
and cook until sausage is lightly browned and
crumbly.

Spoon into a medium-size bowl and add cream
cheese, parsley, mustard and fresh bread
crumbs; mix. Shape into small balls trying to
make the surface smooth. Dip in beaten egg then
roll in dry bread crumbs until evenly coated.
Chill until ready to cook in hot oil.

To make Chutney Sauce, put Tomato Sauce in a
medium-size saucepan and stir in chutney; heat
through. Serve warm. Makes about 4 servings.

Serve Mustard Sauce, page 41, also.

Middle-Eastern Lamb Fondue

1-1/2 lbs. boneless lamb

Marinade:
3 tablespoons olive oil
1 tablespoon lemon juice
1 garlic clove, crushed
1 tablespoon chopped fresh mint
1 teaspoon ground cinnamon
Salt and pepper

Apricot Sauce:
1 tablespoon vegetable oil
1 shallot, finely chopped
1 (16-oz.) can apricots in natural juice
1 tablespoon chopped parsley

Cut lamb in bite-size cubes. Mix marinade ingredients together, pour over lamb and marinate at least 2 hours, but preferably overnight.

To make Apricot Sauce, heat vegetable oil in a medium-size saucepan, add shallot and cook over low heat until soft. Add apricots and their juice and simmer 5 minutes.

Puree sauce in either a blender or food processor. Pour puree back into saucepan, stir in parsley and reheat before serving. Makes 4 to 6 servings.

Serve Cucumber & Yogurt Sauce, page 41, also.

Mexican Beef Fondue

2 lbs. beef tenderloin or sirloin

Mexican Sauce:
1 tablespoon vegetable oil
1/4 cup finely chopped yellow onion
1 garlic clove
1 (16-oz.) can peeled tomatoes
2 tablespoons tomato paste
1/2 teaspoon chili powder
1 green chili, finely chopped
Salt and pepper

Cut meat in 1-inch cubes and put on a serving plate.

To make Mexican Sauce, heat vegetable oil in a medium-size saucepan, add onion and garlic and cook gently until softened. Stir in tomatoes and their juice, tomato paste and chili powder. Simmer uncovered 10 minutes.

Remove sauce from heat and puree in a blender or food processor until smooth, or press through a sieve to give a smooth sauce. Return to heat, add chopped green chili and simmer 15 minutes. Season with salt and pepper to taste. Makes 4 to 6 servings.

Serve Cool Avocado Dip, page 40, also.

Pork Saté

2 lbs. lean boneless pork
1/2 teaspoon chili powder
1 teaspoon ground coriander
1/2 teaspoon turmeric
1 tablespoon vegetable oil
1 tablespoon soy sauce
1/2 teaspoon salt

Peanut-Chili Sauce:
2/3 cup shredded coconut
1-1/4 cups boiling water
5 tablespoons crunchy peanut butter
2 teaspoons sugar
1 green chili, finely chopped
1 teaspoon lemon juice
1 garlic clove, crushed

Cut pork in 3/4-inch cubes.

In a large bowl mix together spices, vegetable oil, soy sauce and salt to make a paste; add pork. With wet hands, knead mixture into pork. Cover bowl and leave at least 2 hours.

To make Peanut-Chili Sauce, put coconut in a medium-size bowl and pour boiling water over. Let stand 15 minutes. Pour through a sieve into a medium-size bowl pressing the liquid through the sieve; discard coconut. Pour liquid into a saucepan. Add remaining ingredients to coconut liquid and mix well. Cook over low heat, stirring until sauce boils. Serve hot. Makes about 6 servings.

Teriyaki Fondue

2 lbs. lean beef tenderloin or sirloin
1 tablespoon brown sugar
1/2 cup soy sauce
6 tablespoons dry sherry
2 garlic cloves, crushed
1 teaspoon ground ginger

Bean Sprout Salad:
1 small head Chinese cabbage
8 oz. bean sprouts, roots trimmed
1 red bell pepper, finely sliced
6 green onions, shredded
6 tablespoons sunflower oil
1 tablespoon wine vinegar

Cut meat in thin strips 1/2 inch wide and 4 inches long.

Put 1 teaspoon brown sugar and 2 tablespoons soy sauce in a small bowl and set aside. In a large bowl combine remaining brown sugar and soy sauce with sherry, garlic and ginger; add meat and marinate 1 hour. Spear meat on bamboo skewers.

To prepare salad, shred Chinese cabbage and put in a salad bowl with bean sprouts, red bell pepper and green onions. Add sunflower oil to reserved sugar and soy sauce mixture and beat in vinegar. Pour over salad and toss together. Makes about 4 to 6 servings.

——— ACCOMPANIMENTS ———

COOL AVOCADO DIP:
1 medium-size avocado
2 teaspoons lemon juice
2/3 cup sour cream
1 teaspoon grated onion
Salt and pepper

To make Cool Avocado Dip, cut avocado in half, discard seed and scoop flesh into a bowl. Mash with lemon juice until smooth then stir in sour cream, onion, salt and pepper. Makes about 1-1/2 cups.

ANCHOVY MAYONNAISE:
1 (1-1/2-oz.) can anchovies, drained
6 tablespoons mayonnaise
2 tablespoons half and half
2 tablespoons olive oil
2 teaspoons tomato paste

To make Anchovy Mayonnaise, place all ingredients in a blender or food processor and process until smooth. Makes about 1 cup.

CREAMY HORSERADISH SAUCE:
2/3 cup whipping cream
1 tablespoon grated fresh horseradish
2 green onions, chopped

To make Creamy Horseradish Sauce, whip cream until soft peaks form then stir in rest of ingredients. Chill before serving. Makes about 3/4 cup.

ACCOMPANIMENTS

CUCUMBER & YOGURT SAUCE:
2 oz. Neufchâtel cheese
2/3 cup plain low-fat yogurt
2/3 cup peeled, finely diced cucumber
2 teaspoons lemon juice
Salt and pepper

To make Cucumber & Yogurt Sauce, beat cheese and yogurt together until smooth. Blend in cucumber, lemon juice, salt and pepper. Makes about 2 cups.

SPICY ORIENTAL SAUCE:
2 tablespoons soy sauce
1-1/2 tablespoons lemon juice
2 green chili peppers, chopped
1 garlic clove, crushed
2 teaspoons sesame oil

To make Spicy Oriental Sauce, put all ingredients in a small bowl and mix together. Makes about 1/2 cup.

MUSTARD SAUCE:
1 tablespoon Dijon mustard
2/3 cup sour cream
3 tablespoons mayonnaise
Salt and pepper

To make Mustard Sauce, put mustard, sour cream and mayonnaise in a small bowl and mix together until smooth. Season with salt and pepper. Makes about 1 cup.

—— Potato Skins with Sour Cream ——

3 lbs. medium-size russet potatoes
5 tablespoons butter, melted
Salt
2/3 cup sour cream
2 tablespoons snipped chives

Preheat oven to 400F (205C). Scrub potatoes and prick with a fork; place in an ovenproof dish. Bake about 1 hour until tender.

Remove potatoes from oven and cut each in quarters. Remove insides leaving about 1/4-inch flesh on inside of skins. (The cooked potato can be used in soups.) Increase oven temperature to 450F (230C).

Brush inside and outside of each potato skin with butter, sprinkle with salt and place on a baking sheet. Bake about 10 minutes or until crisp. Mix sour cream with chives and serve with the cooked potato skins. Makes about 6 servings.

Chinese Fried Rice

2 tablespoons vegetable oil
6 green onions, chopped
1/2 lb. mushrooms, chopped
1/2 red bell pepper, chopped
1/2 green bell pepper, chopped
2-1/2 cups cooked rice
4 oz. cooked peeled prawns
4 oz. cooked ham, diced
1/2 teaspoon ground ginger
1/4 teaspoon cayenne pepper
Salt

Heat oil in a large frying pan; add green onions, mushrooms and peppers and cook 2 minutes.

Add rice and cook 3 minutes, stirring.

Add prawns, ham, spices and salt; continue to cook 3 to 4 minutes. Serve hot. Makes about 6 servings.

Monkfish & Scallop Kabobs

8 large scallops
1-1/4 lbs. monkfish
1/4 cup all-purpose flour seasoned with salt and
   pepper

Tarragon & Wine Sauce:
2 tablespoons butter
1 shallot, finely chopped
2/3 cup dry white wine
2 teaspoons chopped fresh tarragon
Salt and pepper
1/4 cup half and half

Remove coral part of scallops and set aside; cut white part in half.

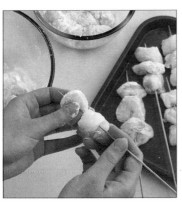

Cut monkfish in bite-size pieces. Toss monkfish and scallops in flour to coat. Spear 1 piece of scallop and 2 pieces of monkfish on each bamboo skewer and set aside until needed. They will be deep-fried in hot oil later.

To make Tarragon & Wine Sauce, melt butter in a small saucepan, add chopped shallot and cook until soft. Add reserved scallop corals and cook over medium heat 5 minutes. Add wine, tarragon, salt and pepper and simmer 5 minutes. Puree sauce in a blender or food processor until smooth, then return to saucepan. Stir in half and half and reheat before serving. Makes about 4 servings.

Crispy Cod Bites

1-1/2 lbs. thick cod fillets, skinned
1/4 cup all-purpose flour seasoned with salt and
** pepper**
2 eggs, lightly beaten
2 cups fresh bread crumbs

Lemon-Parsley Sauce:
2 tablespoons butter
2 tablespoons all-purpose flour
1 cup fish stock or clam juice
Grated peel and juice of 1/2 lemon
1 tablespoon chopped parsley
Salt and pepper
3 tablespoons half and half

Cut fish in bite-size pieces; coat in seasoned flour. Dip fish in beaten egg then roll in bread crumbs and set aside.

To make Lemon-Parsley Sauce, melt butter in a small saucepan, stir in flour and cook 1 minute. Gradually add fish stock or clam juice then bring to a boil and simmer 1 to 2 minutes or until thickened. Stir in lemon peel and juice, parsley, salt and pepper. Heat for 1 minute then add half and half.

Serve warm with fish which is speared on fondue forks and deep-fried in hot oil. Makes about 4 servings.

Serve Thousand Island Sauce, page 49, and Dill Sauce, page 48, also.

Gefilte Fish

1-1/2 lbs. mixed white fish, skinned
1 small onion, quartered
1 egg, beaten
2 tablespoons chopped parsley
1/4 cup ground almonds
4 tablespoons fine matzo meal

Sour Cream & Beet Sauce:
2/3 cup sour cream
1/4 cup canned cubed beets
1 tablespoon prepared horseradish

Chop fish and onion in a food processor. Transfer to a medium-size bowl.

Add rest of ingredients to minced fish, season with salt and pepper and mix. Add a little more matzo meal if a stiffer mixture is desired. With wet hands, form the mixture into 36 smooth small balls. Place on a tray and refrigerate at least 30 minutes before deep-frying in hot oil.

To make Sour Cream & Beet Sauce, put sour cream in a small bowl. Stir in beets and horseradish. Season with salt and pepper. Makes 4 to 6 servings.

Spicy Mediterranean Prawns

1-1/2 lbs. medium-size shrimp
2 tablespoons vegetable oil
1 teaspoon paprika
Dash cayenne pepper
2 teaspoons lemon juice

Piquant Sauce:
1-1/4 cups tomato juice
2 teaspoons brown sugar
2 teaspoons red-wine vinegar
1/4 teaspoon ground cinnamon
1/4 teaspoon ground ginger
1 small red chili, finely chopped

Peel prawns, leaving tails on if desired, and put in a medium-size bowl with rest of ingredients; mix together and leave at least 1 hour.

To make Piquant Sauce, put all ingredients in a small saucepan and simmer 15 minutes.

Before deep-frying prawns in hot oil, drain and arrange on a serving plate. Serve Piquant Sauce hot. Makes 6 servings as an appetizer or 4 servings as a main course.

Almandine Trout

4 trout
1/4 cup all-purpose flour seasoned with salt and
   pepper
2 eggs, lightly beaten
1 cup blanched almonds, lightly toasted and
   finely chopped

Dill Sauce:
4 teaspoons cornstarch
2/3 cup fish stock or clam juice
2/3 cup milk
2 tablespoons chopped fresh dill
Salt and pepper

Clean fish, cut off fins then slice in pieces just under 1/2 inch thick.

Coat pieces of trout in seasoned flour. Dip in egg then roll in chopped almonds. Place on a serving plate and refrigerate until ready to deep-fry in hot oil.

To make Dill Sauce, blend cornstarch with a portion of fish stock in a small saucepan. Add remaining stock and milk; simmer until thickened. Stir in dill, salt and pepper. Serve hot. Makes about 4 servings.

Swordfish Acapulco

1-1/2 lbs. swordfish steaks

Marinade:
4 tablespoons vegetable oil
2/3 cup dry white wine
1 garlic clove, crushed

Thousand Island Sauce:
1 cup mayonnaise
1 teaspoon tomato paste
2 tablespoons chopped stuffed olives
2 tablespoons finely chopped onion
1 hard-boiled egg, chopped
1 tablespoon chopped parsley

Cut fish in bite-size pieces. Mix marinade ingredients together, season with salt and pepper then stir in fish; leave 2 to 3 hours

To make Thousand Island Sauce, put all ingredients in a small bowl and mix together. Season with salt and pepper, then spoon into a serving dish.

Before deep-frying fish in hot oil, drain from marinade and put in a serving dish. Makes 4 to 6 servings.

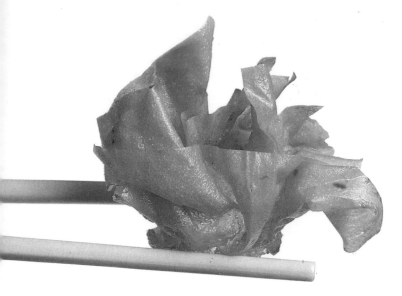

Wafer-Wrapped Prawns

3/4 lb. peeled prawns, roughly chopped
1 green chili, finely chopped
2 teaspoons oyster sauce
2 sheets filo pastry

Chili Sauce:
1/4 cup ketchup
1 to 2 teaspoons chili sauce
2 tablespoons water
1/2 teaspoon sesame oil

In a bowl mix prawns, green chili and oyster sauce together.

Cut filo pastry in 4-inch squares. Place a heaped teaspoon of prawn filling in the center of each square, draw the corners of pastry together and twist them to form a small package. Place on a floured serving plate and chill until ready to use. The best way to cook the packages is for each person to use a small Chinese wire strainer to lift them out of the hot oil.

To make Chili Sauce, put all ingredients in a small saucepan and cook over medium heat 3 to 4 minutes. Serve hot. Makes 24.

Alternatively serve Deviled Sauce, page 29.

Seafood Tempura

1/2 lb. scampi tails, thawed if frozen
4 small squid, cut in rings
4 flounder fillets, skinned
1/2 lb. halibut, skinned
1/2 lb. salmon, skinned

Tempura Dipping Sauce:
2 tablespoons dry sherry
2 tablespoons soy sauce
1 cup chicken broth

Garnish:
1 tablespoon grated ginger root
1/2 lb. daikon (mooli) or turnip, grated

Batter:
See page 56 for ingredients; increase water to
   3/4 cup

Cut white fish in thin slices or fingers. Arrange all seafood on a flat serving platter.

Mix together all ingredients for Tempura Dipping Sauce and place in a serving bowl. Prepare garnish by mixing ginger and daikon together.

To make batter, sift flour and salt into a bowl. Beat in egg yolks and olive oil. Gradually add 3/4 cup water and continue to beat to make a smooth batter. Set aside 1 hour. Just before serving, beat egg whites until stiff and fold them into the batter. Set bowl of batter inside a second ice-cube-filled bowl. Each person spears a piece of fish with a fondue fork, dips it in the batter then deep-fries it in the hot oil. The cooked food is dipped in the sauce and eaten with the garnish. Makes 4 to 6 servings.

Serve Chili Sauce, page 50, and Spicy Oriental Sauce, page 41, also.

Cauliflower Fritters

1 lb. cauliflower, cut in florets
3/4 cup dry bread crumbs
1/3 cup (1 oz.) grated Parmesan cheese
1 tablespoon chopped parsley
2 to 3 eggs, lightly beaten

Cheese Sauce:
1 tablespoon butter
2 tablespoons all-purpose flour
1-1/4 cups milk
1/2 teaspoon prepared mustard
1/2 cup (1-1/2 oz.) shredded Cheddar cheese
Dash cayenne pepper
Salt and pepper

Boil cauliflower in 1/2 cup water 4 to 5 minutes, drain well.

Combine bread crumbs, Parmesan cheese and parsley together; season with salt and pepper. Dip cauliflower florets in beaten egg, coat in bread crumb mixture and place on a serving plate. Set aside.

To make Cheese Sauce, melt butter in a small saucepan, stir in flour and cook 1 minute. Remove from heat and stir in milk gradually. Bring to a boil and simmer 2 minutes. Add mustard, cheese, cayenne, salt and pepper; heat just until cheese melts. Serve hot. Makes 4 to 6 servings.

Alternatively serve Piquant Sauce, page 47.

Mixed Vegetable Kabobs

4 medium-size zucchini
16 medium-size mushrooms
1 red bell pepper, cut in chunks
1 green bell pepper, cut in chunks

Creamy Onion Sauce:
2 oz. Neufchâtel cheese
2/3 cup plain low-fat yogurt
6 green onions, finely chopped

Batter:
2 large eggs
1 cup all-purpose flour

Spear vegetables on bamboo skewers.

To make Creamy Onion Sauce, mix all in-gredients together and put in a serving bowl.

Just before cooking the kabobs, prepare batter. Put eggs in a medium-size bowl with 3/4 cup iced water and beat until frothy. Add flour and beat just until blended (do not worry if a few lumps are left). Pour into a dish set in a bowl of ice.

To cook kabobs, each person dips the skewered vegetables in the batter then in the hot oil to deep-fry until the batter is golden. The kabobs are then eaten with the sauce. Makes about 4 servings.

Serve Fresh Tomato Sauce, page 54, also.

Spicy Chickpea Balls

3/4 cup bulgur wheat
1/2 lb. chickpeas, soaked in water overnight
2 garlic cloves, crushed
1/2 teaspoon baking powder
1 teaspoon chili powder
1 teaspoon ground coriander
1 teaspoon ground cumin
2 tablespoons sunflower oil

Fresh Tomato Sauce:
4 medium-size tomatoes, skinned
1/2 green bell pepper
1/2 red bell pepper
1 green chili
1 tablespoon fresh coriander, chopped

Put wheat in a medium-size bowl and pour 1/2 cup boiling water over. Soak 1 hour. Drain chickpeas and place in a food processor with wheat and rest of ingredients. Season with salt and pepper. Blend a few minutes until mixture becomes fairly smooth. With your hands mold the mixture into about 36 small balls; place on a serving dish. These will be speared with a fondue fork and deep-fried in hot oil.

To make Fresh Tomato Sauce, put all ingredients in a blender or food processor and process until vegetables are finely chopped. Place sauce in a serving bowl. Makes 4 to 6 servings.

Swiss Potatoes

2 lbs. small new potatoes, scrubbed
2 eggs, lightly beaten
1 cup herb-seasoned stuffing mix

Garlic Sauce:
2 cups fresh white bread crumbs
2 garlic cloves
1/2 teaspoon salt
1 cup olive oil
4 teaspoons lemon juice
1 tablespoon white-wine vinegar

Boil potatoes just until tender, drain and allow
to cool. Dip in beaten egg then roll in stuffing
mix; place on a plate and set aside. These will be
speared with a fondue fork and deep-fried in hot
oil.

To make Garlic Sauce, dampen bread crumbs
with water. Put in a blender or food processor
with garlic and salt; puree. Add olive oil a little
at a time and continue to process until it has all
been added.

Add lemon juice and vinegar to the sauce and
process until it is a smooth and creamy consistency. Pour sauce into a serving bowl and
serve with potatoes. Makes 4 to 6 servings.

Serve Cheese Sauce, page 52, also.

Eggplant Fritters

1 lb. eggplant, diced
Salt
2 tablespoons all-purpose flour
Salt and pepper

Batter:
1 cup all-purpose flour
1/4 teaspoon salt
2 eggs, separated
2 tablespoons olive oil
1/4 cup water

Cool Curry Sauce:
2 teaspoons curry paste
1 teaspoon Dijon mustard
2 teaspoons brown sugar
4 teaspoons grated onion
6 tablespoons mayonnaise
6 tablespoons plain low-fat yogurt

Put eggplant in a colander, sprinkle with salt and leave to drain 30 minutes.

To make batter, sift flour and salt into a medium-size bowl. Beat in egg yolks and olive oil. Gradually add water and continue to beat to make a smooth batter. Let stand 1 hour. Just before serving, beat egg whites until stiff then fold into batter.

To make Cool Curry Sauce, beat all ingredients together in a small bowl then spoon into a serving dish. Rinse eggplant, dry thoroughly on paper towels and dust with flour, salt and pepper. To cook fritters, each piece of eggplant is speared on a fondue fork, dipped in the batter then deep-fried in the fondue pot. Makes about 4 servings.

Serve Garlic Sauce, page 55, also.

– Cantonese Chrysanthemum Hotpot –

1/2 lb. beef round steak, fat removed
3/4 lb. boned chicken breasts, skinned
1/2 lb. peeled prawns
1/4 lb. Chinese pea pods
1 red bell pepper, cut in strips
1/4 lb. mushrooms, halved
1 (8-oz.) can bamboo shoots, drained
6 cups chicken broth
2 teaspoons chopped ginger root
2 oz. dry ramen noodles, broken up

Yellow Bean Sauce:
1 tablespoon soy sauce
2 tablespoons yellow bean sauce
1 tablespoon dry sherry
1 green chili, finely chopped
2 tablespoons water

Slice steak and chicken thinly; arrange these and prawns on 6 individual plates with the vegetables. Put broth in a medium-size saucepan with ginger and simmer. Soak egg noodles in warm water 10 minutes, drain and put in a serving bowl. Combine ingredients for Yellow Bean Sauce; divide sauce between 6 small dishes.

Pour broth into fondue pot and bring to the burner at the table simmering. Each person uses a fondue fork or Chinese wire strainer to deep-fry pieces of food in the broth then dips the cooked food in the sauce before eating. When all the meat and vegetables are eaten, add the noodles to the fondue pot to heat through. Then ladle the soup into bowls. Makes 4 to 6 servings.

Serve Ginger Sauce, page 59, also.

Chinese Seafood Hotpot

6 fresh king-size prawns
6 scallops, sliced
4 small squid, cut in rings
3 lemon sole fillets, skinned
4 trout fillets, skinned
6 cups chicken broth
1 teaspoon sliced ginger root
4 green onions, chopped
2 oz. transparent rice noodles
1 lb. Chinese cabbage, finely shredded

Hoisin Sauce:
2 tablespoons Hoisin sauce
1 tablespoon ketchup
2 teaspoons soy sauce

Cut white fish in thin strips; arrange on a platter with other fish. Put broth in a medium-size saucepan with ginger and green onions and simmer 15 minutes. Mix the ingredients for Hoisin Sauce together; divide into 6 small dishes. Soak rice noodles in water 5 minutes then cut in short lengths; place in a serving bowl. Place shredded cabbage in a bowl.

Strain broth into fondue pot on the stove. Once broth begins to simmer again, place fondue pot over the burner at the table. Arrange the platter of fish, Hoisin Sauce, noodles and cabbage on the table. The fish and cabbage are deep-fried in the hot broth using Chinese wire strainers to hold the food. Any remaining cabbage can be added at the end with the noodles to make the soup. Makes about 6 servings.

Serve Ginger Sauce, page 59, also.

—— Thai Meat Balls & Fish Balls ——

Ginger Sauce:
2 teaspoons chopped ginger root
2 tablespoons dry sherry or rice wine
2 tablespoons soy sauce

Meat Balls:
3 dried mushrooms, soaked in water 30 minutes
1 lb. lean ground beef
1 tablespoon chopped fresh coriander
2 green onions, finely chopped
1 tablespoon rice wine

Fish Balls:
1 (3-1/2-oz.) can shrimp, drained
1-1/2 lbs. cod or haddock fillets, skinned
1 teaspoon finely grated ginger root
1 tablespoon cornstarch

4 cups chicken broth

Mix together ingredients for Ginger Sauce. To make meat balls, squeeze water from mushrooms and chop. Combine with remaining ingredients; season with salt and pepper. Form into 18 small balls.

To make fish balls, chop shrimp and cod in a food processor. Stir in ginger and cornstarch. Form into 24 small balls.

Bring chicken broth to a boil in the fondue pot over the stove; transfer pot to the burner at the table. To cook the meat balls and fish balls in the broth use fondue forks or Chinese wire strainers. Makes about 6 servings.

Golden Vegetable Puree

1/2 lb. carrots
1 small turnip
1/2 medium-size rutabaga
2 celery stalks
1 small onion
1-1/4 cups chicken broth
1/4 cup butter
Salt and pepper
Dash nutmeg

To Serve:
small cooked sausages and cooked potatoes

Chop all vegetables finely; put in a medium-size saucepan with broth. Bring to a boil then simmer just until vegetables are tender.

Drain vegetables and let cool slightly. Puree in a blender or food processor. Pour puree through a sieve into fondue pot.

Place fondue pot over low heat on stove and gradually beat in butter, salt, pepper and nutmeg. Transfer fondue pot to the burner at the table. Serve with small cooked sausages and potatoes. Makes 4 to 6 servings.

Mushroom Fondue

1/4 cup butter
1 lb. mushrooms, finely chopped
2 garlic cloves, crushed
2/3 cup chicken broth
2/3 cup whipping cream
1 tablespoon cornstarch
Salt and pepper
Dash cayenne pepper

To Serve:
cubes of cheese and thick-sliced cold cuts

Melt butter in a medium-size saucepan, add mushrooms and garlic and sauté over medium heat 10 minutes.

Add broth and simmer 10 minutes. Cool slightly then puree in a blender or food processor.

Blend a portion of the whipping cream with cornstarch in fondue pot. Stir in rest of whipping cream and mushroom puree. Simmer over medium heat until thickened. Season with salt, pepper and cayenne. Serve with cubes of cheese and cold cuts. Makes 4 to 6 servings.

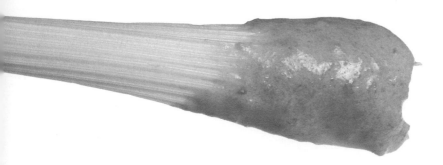

Tomato Niçoise Fondue

1/4 cup butter
1-1/2 lbs. tomatoes, quartered
1 garlic clove, crushed
1 small onion, chopped
1 (6-oz.) can pimientos, drained and chopped
2 tablespoons mayonnaise

To Serve:
cooked artichoke leaves, cooked green beans, strips of cucumber and celery

Melt butter in a medium-size saucepan, add tomatoes, garlic, onion and pimientos and cook over medium heat 10 to 15 minutes or until soft.

Press mixture through a sieve into a bowl, season with salt, pepper and a dash of sugar and allow to cool. Blend in mayonnaise.

Pour Tomato Niçoise into a serving bowl, place on a large platter and arrange vegetables around. Makes about 4 servings.

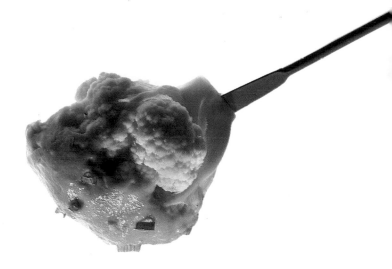

Leek Puree

2 lbs. leeks, roughly chopped
2/3 cup chicken broth
1/4 cup butter
Salt and pepper
Dash nutmeg
2 tablespoons finely chopped green onions

To Serve:
raw cauliflower florets, carrot sticks, mushrooms

Wash leeks well, put in a medium-size saucepan with a little water and simmer 10 to 15 minutes or until soft.

Drain leeks and allow to cool slightly. In a blender or food processor puree leeks with broth.

Spoon puree into a fondue pot and place over medium heat on the stove. Beat in butter; season with salt, pepper and nutmeg. Stir in green onions then place over burner on the table to keep warm. Serve with a selection of raw vegetables or serve with barbecued meat. Makes 4 to 6 servings.

Creamy Corn Fondue

1 (16-oz.) pkg. frozen whole-kernel corn
2 teaspoons cornstarch
3 tablespoons half and half
Salt and pepper
Tabasco sauce
2 tablespoons butter

To Serve:
selection of cooked shellfish

Put corn in a medium-size saucepan with a little water and simmer a few minutes until tender.

Drain corn, put in a blender or food processor and process until soft but not too smooth. In a medium-size saucepan blend cornstarch with half and half, add corn puree and cook over low heat until smooth.

Pour into fondue pot, season with salt, pepper and a few drops Tabasco sauce. Beat in butter. Set fondue pot over burner at the table and serve with a selection of cooked shellfish such as prawns and mussles. Makes 4 to 6 servings.

Spicy Black-Eyed Pea Dip

1 cup black-eyed peas, soaked in water
   overnight
1 garlic clove
A few sprigs parsley
1/2 teaspoon salt
1/4 cup butter
1 medium-size onion, chopped
1 teaspoon curry paste
2/3 cup plain low-fat yogurt

Curried Bread Cubes:
1 small loaf white bread
Vegetable oil
1 tablespoon curry powder

Drain peas and place in a medium-size saucepan. Add enough fresh water to cover the peas, then add garlic clove and parsley. Simmer about 1 hour or until peas are tender. Stir salt into beans and cook 5 minutes; drain and remove parsley. In a small saucepan, melt butter and cook onion until tender. Put beans and onion in a blender or food processor and puree. Pour bean puree into fondue pot, stir in curry paste and yogurt and reheat.

To make Curried Bread Cubes, cut crust off loaf, then cut bread in 1-inch cubes. Heat oil to 350F (175C) and fry cubes in oil until crisp and golden, about 65 seconds. Drain on paper towels. Sprinkle curry powder over and toss together to coat. Spear bread cubes with fondue forks and dip in bean fondue. Makes 4 to 6 servings.

Strawberry Roule Dip

1 (16-oz.) can strawberries, drained
8 oz. strawberry roule cheese
2/3 cup whipping cream

To Serve:
fresh strawberries and Quick Almond Cake, page 69

Put canned strawberries and cheese in a blender or food processor and blend until smooth.

Whip cream until soft peaks form then fold in strawberry-cheese mixture. Spoon into a serving bowl.

Hull fresh strawberries and arrange on a plate with cubes of Quick Almond Cake. Spear on fondue forks and dip. Makes 4 to 6 servings.

Raspberry Cream

1 lb. raspberries, thawed if frozen
4 teaspoons cornstarch
1-1/4 cups half and half
1/3 cup powdered sugar
3 tablespoons framboise (optional)

Quick Meringues:
2 egg whites
2/3 cup powdered sugar

Push raspberries through a sieve and discard seeds; set puree aside.

To make Quick Meringues, preheat oven to 325F (165C). Line a baking sheet with waxed paper. Place egg whites and powdered sugar in a bowl over a pan of hot water. With an electric mixer, beat the mixture until stiff peaks form. Spoon mixture into a piping bag fitted with a 1/2-inch-star tip and pipe small shapes onto prepared baking sheet. Bake 10 to 15 minutes or until crisp on the outside. Allow to cool before removing from waxed paper.

In a medium-size saucepan, blend cornstarch with a small portion of half and half. Stir in remaining half and half, sugar and raspberry puree; cook over medium heat until smooth and thickened. Stir in framboise. Pour into fondue pot and serve, hot or cold, with meringues. Makes 4 to 6 servings.

Serve pieces of fresh fruit to dip also.

Spiced Plum Puree

1-1/2 lbs. red plums
1/2 cup sugar
1/2 teaspoon ground cinnamon
1-1/4 cups water
4 teaspoons cornstarch
2 tablespoons ginger wine

To Serve:
slices of apple and pear; Lemon Cake, page 105

Cut plums in half, discard seeds and put in a medium-size saucepan with sugar, cinnamon and water. Cover and simmer 15 minutes.

Press through a sieve into fondue pot.

In a small bowl blend cornstarch with wine. Stir into plum puree and cook over medium heat until thickened. Serve small squares of Lemon Cake and slices of apple and pear to dip in the puree. Makes 4 to 6 servings.

Apricot-Yogurt Dip

8 oz. whole dried apricots
1-1/4 cups water
2 tablespoons Amaretto liqueur
2/3 cup plain low-fat yogurt

Quick Almond Cake:
2 eggs
1/2 cup margarine, softened
1/2 cup sugar
1 cup self-rising flour
Dash baking powder
A few drops almond extract

Soak apricots in water 2 to 3 hours.

To make Quick Almond Cake, preheat oven to 350F (175C). Grease an 8-inch-square cake pan. Put all ingredients in a medium size bowl and beat together 3 minutes. Pour into prepared pan and bake 25 minutes or until golden and firm to the touch. Cool on a wire rack; cut in small squares.

Drain apricots and place in a blender or food processor with Amaretto and yogurt; blend until smooth. If mixture is too thick add a small amount of the liquid in which the apricots were soaked. Spoon apricot mixture into fondue pot and heat on the stove. Once heated, set fondue pot over burner at the table. Serve with squares of cake. Makes 4 to 6 servings.

——— Gooseberry & Wine Fondue ———

1-1/2 lbs. gooseberries, trimmed
1/2 cup sugar
2/3 cup dry white wine
2 teaspoons cornstarch
2 tablespoons half and half

Brandy Snaps:
1/4 cup butter
1/3 cup packed brown sugar
2 tablespoons light corn syrup
1/2 cup all-purpose flour
1/2 teaspoon ground ginger

To make Brandy Snaps, preheat oven to 350F (175C). Melt butter, brown sugar and corn syrup in a small saucepan. Cool slightly then beat in flour and ginger. Place heaping table-spoonfuls of mixture on ungreased baking sheets, spacing about 1 inch apart. Bake 10 minutes. Cool slightly before removing with a small knife and rolling each cookie around the handle of a wooden spoon or wooden chopstick. Allow cookie to set before removing from spoon handle. Makes about 2 dozen Brandy Snaps.

Reserve a few gooseberries for decoration. Put remaining gooseberries in a medium-size sauce-pan with sugar and wine. Simmer until tender then press through a sieve to make a puree. In a fondue pot blend cornstarch with half and half, stir in gooseberry puree and heat until smooth and thick. Decorate with reserved gooseberries and serve with Brandy Snaps. Makes 4 to 6 servings.

—— Blackcurrant Cassis Fondue ——

1-1/2 lbs. blackcurrants, thawed if frozen
1/2 cup sugar
2/3 cup water
1 tablespoon cornstarch
2 tablespoons half and half
1/4 cup crème de cassis

Hazelnut Cookies:
2 egg whites
1/2 cup packed brown sugar
1-2/3 cups ground hazelnuts
1/4 cup finely chopped hazelnuts

To make cookies, preheat oven to 350F (175C). Line two baking sheets with waxed paper. Beat egg whites until soft peaks form. Fold in brown sugar and ground hazelnuts.

Place teaspoonfuls of mixture on prepared baking sheets and sprinkle with chopped hazelnuts. Bake 15 to 20 minutes or until crisp and firm to the touch. Makes about 2 dozen cookies.

To make fondue, place blackcurrants in a medium-size saucepan with sugar and water. Cook over medium heat until tender. Press through a sieve into fondue pot. In a small bowl blend cornstarch with half and half; stir into puree with crème de cassis and reheat until thickened. When ready to serve, swirl a little extra cream in for decoration. Serve with Hazelnut Cookies. Makes 4 to 6 servings.

Butterscotch Fondue

1/4 cup butter
3/4 cup packed brown sugar
1/4 cup light corn syrup
1 (14-oz.) can evaporated milk
1/4 cup chopped unsalted peanuts
2 tablespoons cornstarch

To Serve:
popcorn; cubes of apple, pear and banana

Put butter, sugar and corn syrup in a medium-size saucepan and heat until mixture begins to bubble; boil 1 minute.

Stir in evaporated milk and cook 3 to 4 minutes or until sauce is hot and bubbly. Add chopped peanuts.

In a small bowl, blend cornstarch with 2 table-spoons water. Add to sauce and heat until thickened. Pour sauce into fondue pot and place over burner at the table. Serve with popcorn, cubes of apple, pear and banana. Makes 4 to 6 servings.

Peppermint Fondue

1-1/4 pints half and half
1 cup powdered sugar
2 tablespoons cornstarch
Peppermint extract to taste

Mini-Chocolate Cakes:
2 eggs
1/2 cup margarine, softened
1/2 cup sugar
1 cup self-rising flour
2 tablespoons cocoa
1 tablespoon milk

To make Mini-Chocolate Cakes, preheat oven to 375F (190C). Put all ingredients in a medium-size bowl and beat together until smooth.

Place teaspoonfuls of batter in miniature paper baking cups and bake 15 minutes or until cooked. Cool on a wire rack before removing the paper cups. Makes about 3-1/2 dozen cakes.

To make fondue, put half and half and sugar in a medium-size saucepan. Heat until almost boiling. Blend cornstarch with a little water and stir into mixture. Continue to heat, stirring, until thickened; add peppermint extract. Pour into fondue pot and serve hot with Mini-Chocolate Cakes. Makes about 6 servings.

Chocolate-Nut Fondue

12 oz. Swiss chocolate bar with nuts
1 cup whipping cream
2 tablespoons brandy or rum

Viennese Fingers:
1/2 cup butter
2 tablespoons powdered sugar
1 cup all-purpose flour
1/4 teaspoon baking powder
A few drops vanilla extract

To Serve:
selection of fruit

To make Viennese Fingers, preheat oven to 375F (190C). Grease two baking sheets. Beat butter and powdered sugar together until pale and creamy.

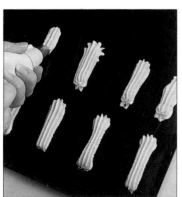

Sift in flour and baking powder; beat well. Mix in vanilla extract. Spoon mixture into a piping bag fitted with a 1/4-inch-star tip and pipe 2-inch fingers onto prepared baking sheets. Bake 15 minutes. Cool on wire rack. Makes about 2 dozen fingers.

To make Chocolate-Nut Fondue, break up chocolate and place in fondue pot. Add whipping cream and heat slowly, stirring constantly, until chocolate melts. Stir in brandy. Place fondue pot over burner at the table and serve with Viennese Fingers and fruit. Makes 6 servings.

Mocha Fondue

8 oz. semisweet chocolate
1 tablespoon instant coffee granules
2/3 cup whipping cream
3 tablespoons Tia Maria

Nutty Meringues:
2 egg whites
1/2 cup sugar
2 oz. flaked almonds, lightly toasted

To Serve:
selection of fresh fruit

To make Nutty Meringues, preheat oven to
225F (105C). Line two baking sheets with
waxed paper. Beat egg whites until stiff; fold in
half of sugar and beat again until stiff. Fold in
remaining sugar.

Place teaspoonfuls of mixture on prepared baking sheets, insert a few almonds in each, and
bake 1-1/2 to 2 hours or until dry and crisp. At
the end of the baking time, turn off oven, leaving meringues inside to cool. When cooled, peel
meringues off paper. Makes about 2-1/2 dozen
meringues.

To make Mocha Fondue, break up chocolate
and place in fondue pot. Add coffee granules
and whipping cream and heat slowly until
melted, stirring constantly. Stir in Tia Maria and
beat until smooth. Place over burner at the table
and serve with Nutty Meringues and fruit.
Makes about 6 servings.

Praline Fondue

1/2 cup sugar
3/4 cup whole blanched almonds
8 oz. white chocolate
2/3 cup whipping cream
A few drops almond extract

To Serve:
cubes of cake and selection of fresh fruit

Grease one baking sheet. Put sugar and almonds in a small heavy saucepan. Place over low heat until sugar becomes liquid and golden. Pour onto prepared baking sheet and let cool and harden 15 minutes.

Break up praline into rough pieces and place in a blender or food processor; grind finely.

Put white chocolate and whipping cream in fondue pot and melt over medium heat, stirring constantly. Stir in praline and flavor with almond extract. Serve with cubes of cake and pieces of fresh fruit. Makes about 6 servings.

Fruit Surprises

12 oz. frozen puff pastry, thawed
1 (8-oz.) can pineapple slices, juice reserved
1/3 cup chopped glacé cherries
1 oz. angelica, chopped

Rum Sauce:
4 medium-size oranges
1 tablespoon cornstarch
1/3 cup packed brown sugar
2 tablespoons butter
1/4 cup dark rum

Roll out puff pastry to a large square then cut in 3-inch squares.

Chop pineapple and mix with cherries and angelica in a small bowl. Place one teaspoonful of fruit in the center of each pastry square. Dampen the pastry edges and fold over in triangles and seal well. Refrigerate until needed. Makes 1-1/2 dozen Fruit Surprises.

To make Rum Sauce, grate the peel from one of the oranges, then squeeze the juice from all of them. Put cornstarch in a small saucepan, add reserved pineapple juice and brown sugar and blend together. Pour in orange juice. Bring to a boil, stirring constantly, and simmer 2 minutes. Beat in butter, orange peel and rum and serve hot with Fruit Surprises. The pastry triangles are deep-fried in hot oil in the fondue pot. It is easiest to lift them out with Chinese wire strainers. Makes about 6 servings.

Fruit Fritters

2 medium-size bananas, cut in 1-inch pieces
2 medium-size apples, cut in chunks
Lemon juice
1 small fresh pineapple, skinned and cut in
    chunks

Batter:
1 cup all-purpose flour
Dash salt
1 egg
2/3 cup milk

To Serve:
1/2 cup sugar mixed with 1 teaspoon cinnamon

Toss bananas and apples in lemon juice; arrange on a serving plate with pineapple.

To make batter, sift flour and salt into a bowl. Beat in egg then gradually add milk to make a smooth batter.

The fritters are cooked at the table by spearing the fruit with a fondue fork, dipping it in batter then deep-frying it in hot oil in the fondue pot. Drain each fritter on paper towels, then dip in cinnamon sugar before eating. Makes about 4 servings.

Hot Berry Compote

**1 lb. mixed summer fruits (red currants,
   blackcurrants and raspberries)**
1/2 cup sugar
2/3 cup water
2 tablespoons cornstarch

Langue De Chat Cookies:
1/2 cup butter
1/2 cup sugar
2 eggs
1-1/2 cups self-rising flour

To make cookies, preheat oven to 425F (220C).
Line two baking sheets with waxed paper.
Cream butter and sugar together in a medium-
size bowl until pale and fluffy. Beat in egg and
then flour.

Fill a piping bag fitted with a 1/2-inch-plain tip
with mixture. Pipe 2-1/2-inch fingers on prepared baking sheets. Bake about 8 minutes or
until light golden. Cool on wire rack. Makes
about 2 to 2-1/2 dozen cookies.

To make fondue, put fruit in a medium-size
saucepan with sugar and water and cook over
medium heat until tender. Crush fruit slightly
with a potato masher. In a small bowl, blend
cornstarch with a little water; add to fruit and
cook until thickened. Pour into fondue pot and
place over burner at the table. Serve with cookies. Makes about 6 servings.

Sweet Cherry Compote

2 (16-oz.) cans red cherries
2 tablespoons cornstarch
1/3 cup sugar
3 tablespoons cherry brandy

Fancy Cakes:
1/4 cup butter
2 eggs, separated
1/4 cup sugar
1/2 cup all-purpose flour
1 teaspoon grated lemon peel

To Serve:
ice cream

To make cakes, preheat oven to 375F (190C). Grease and flour a fluted muffin pan. Warm butter in a small saucepan until very soft and just beginning to melt.

Beat egg yolks and sugar until pale and creamy. Fold in flour, lemon peel and butter until thoroughly mixed. Beat egg whites until stiff and fold into batter. Spoon mixture into prepared muffin pan and bake 10 minutes or until golden and firm to the touch. Remove cakes from pan; cool on a wire rack. Makes 1 dozen cakes.

To make compote, drain cherries, reserving juice; remove pits.In a medium-size saucepan, blend cornstarch with a portion of the reserved juice, then add remaining juice with sugar. Cook over medium heat until sauce thickens. Stir in cherries and brandy and reheat. Pour into fondue pot. Using a small ladle, spoon sauce over ice cream and Fancy Cakes. Makes about 6 servings.

Marshmallow Cream Fondue

2 tablespoons cornstarch
1 pint half and half
1 (6-oz.) pkg. marshmallows

Crispy Chocolate Cookies:
1/4 cup butter
2 tablespoons light corn syrup
1/2 cup sweetened cocoa mix
1/3 cup puffed rice cereal

To make Crispy Chocolate Cookies, place butter and corn syrup in a small saucepan and stir over low heat until butter melts. Remove from heat and stir in cocoa mix and cereal. Mix well to coat cereal.

Using a teaspoon, spoon the mixture into miniature paper baking cups and refrigerate to set. Makes about 5 dozen cookies.

To make Marshmallow Cream Fondue, blend cornstarch with a portion of half and half in a medium-size saucepan. Stir in remaining half and half and marshmallows. Cook over medium heat, stirring constantly, until mixture thickens and marshmallows melt. Pour into fondue pot and serve hot with Crispy Chocolate Cookies. Makes 6 to 8 servings.

Coconut Dip

1 cup finely flaked coconut
2 cups water
1/4 cup sugar
1/4 cup cream of coconut
2 teaspoons cornstarch
2/3 cup half and half

Almond Clusters:
1/2 cup margarine
1/4 cup clear honey
1/2 cup packed brown sugar
2 cups rolled oats
1/3 cup chopped almonds

To make Almond Clusters, preheat oven to 350F (175C). In a medium-size saucepan melt margarine with honey and brown sugar. Stir in rolled oats and almonds; mix well.

Spoon mixture into miniature paper baking cups then place on a baking sheet. Bake 20 minutes or until golden; cool. Makes about 3 dozen Almond Clusters.

To make Coconut Dip, place flaked coconut, water, sugar and cream of coconut in a medium-size saucepan. Bring to a boil and simmer 10 minutes. Pour coconut mixture through a sieve into a bowl, pressing the liquid through. In a fondue pot blend cornstarch with half and half; add coconut liquid and cook over medium heat until thickened. Serve with Almond Clusters. Makes about 6 servings.

Sabayon Sauce

4 large ripe firm dessert pears
1/2 cup Marsala
3 egg yolks
1/3 cup sugar
1 tablespoon brandy

Preheat oven to 350F (175C). Peel, halve and core pears; slice thick. Place in an ovenproof dish and pour Marsala over pears. Cover and bake 20 minutes.

Drain juice from the baked pears and reserve. Place egg yolks and sugar in a small bowl and beat until pale and frothy. Add juice from pears then place bowl over a pan of simmering water and beat until the mixture thickens.

Pour sauce into fondue pot and stir in brandy. Serve immediately with the baked pears. Makes about 4 servings.

Shrimp Dip

1 (7-oz.) can shrimp, drained
1/2 (8-oz.) pkg. cream cheese, room
    temperature
1/4 cup mayonnaise
1 small garlic clove, crushed
1 tablespoon white wine
1 teaspoon lemon juice
1 tablespoon snipped chives

To Serve:
small savory crackers

Finely chop shrimp.

Beat together cream cheese and mayonnaise in a medium-size bowl; add garlic, wine and lemon juice.

Stir in shrimp and chives. Spoon into a serving bowl and serve with small savory crackers. Makes about 6 servings.

Aioli

4 garlic cloves
1/4 teaspoon salt
2 egg yolks
1-1/4 cups olive oil
1 tablespoon lemon juice
Pepper

To Serve:
a selection of fresh vegetables

In a small bowl crush garlic cloves with salt to form a pulp. Add egg yolks and beat well.

Gradually beat in olive oil, drop by drop. When the mixture starts to get creamy and smooth, add the oil in a slow, steady stream. Continue beating until thick. Add lemon juice and pepper.

Spoon into a serving bowl and garnish with chopped fresh parsley. Cut vegetables in thin strips or chunks and arrange them around the bowl. Makes about 6 servings.

Guacamole

2 medium-size avocados
3 tablespoons lime juice
1 garlic clove, crushed
2 tomatoes, skinned and finely chopped
3 green onions, finely chopped
1 green chili, finely chopped
1 tablespoon chopped fresh coriander
Salt and pepper

To Serve:
corn or tortilla chips

Cut avocados in half, remove seeds and scoop flesh into a small bowl. Mash together with lime juice.

Add remaining ingredients and stir together.

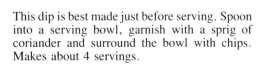

This dip is best made just before serving. Spoon into a serving bowl, garnish with a sprig of coriander and surround the bowl with chips. Makes about 4 servings.

Tapenade Dip

1 (4-1/2-oz.) can pitted black olives
1 (1-3/4-oz.) can anchovies, rinsed and drained
2 tablespoons capers
2 teaspoons lemon juice
2 teaspoons brandy
1/2 teaspoon Dijon mustard
1/4 cup olive oil

To Serve:
thin slices of toast

Put olives, anchovies, capers, lemon juice, brandy and mustard in a blender or food processor; process until a smooth paste forms.

Continue to process the paste while gradually adding olive oil in a steady stream to give a smooth consistency

Spoon dip into a serving dish, garnish with a sprig of parsley and serve with thin slices of toast. Makes about 6 servings.

Bagna Cauda

2 (1-3/4-oz.) cans anchovies, drained
3 garlic cloves
3/4 cup butter
6 tablespoons olive oil
Pepper

To Serve:
a selection of raw or lightly cooked vegetables;
breadsticks

Put anchovies in a small bowl with garlic and mash to make a paste. Alternatively, put anchovies and garlic in a blender or food processor and puree.

Heat butter and oil in a small saucepan until butter melts. Beat into the anchovy paste to give a smooth consistency. Add pepper.

Pour into a small fondue pot and serve with a selection of raw or lightly cooked vegetables and breadsticks. Makes about 6 servings.

Crab & Cheese Dip

4 oz. Neufchâtel cheese
1/2 cup (2 oz.) finely shredded Cheddar cheese
1 teaspoon lemon juice
A few drops Tabasco sauce
1 tablespoon ketchup
3 tablespoons half and half
1 (7-oz.) can crabmeat, drained

Cheese Twists:
1 cup all-purpose flour
A dash each salt, cayenne pepper and dry
   mustard
1/4 cup margarine, softened
1/2 cup (2 oz.) shredded sharp Cheddar cheese
1 egg yolk
1 egg, lightly beaten
Grated Parmesan cheese

Mix together all ingredients for Crab & Cheese Dip and chill. To make Cheese Twists, sift dry ingredients into a bowl. Blend in margarine; add cheese. Beat egg yolk with 1 tablespoon water, add to mixture and mix to form a dough. Knead lightly; chill 30 minutes.

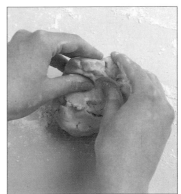

Preheat oven to 350F (175C). Grease two baking sheets. Roll out dough to a rectangle 1/4 inch thick. Brush with beaten egg, sprinkle with Parmesan cheese and cut in strips 1/4 inch wide and 4 inches long. Twist the two ends of each strip and place them on prepared baking sheets. Bake 10 to 12 minutes or until golden brown. Cool on a wire rack and serve with Crab & Cheese Dip. The dip can be garnished with a sprig of fennel, if desired. Makes about 6 servings.

Mongolian Hotpot

3 lbs. lean lamb leg or fillet
6 cups chicken broth
1 teaspoon grated ginger root
1 garlic clove
2 tablespoons chopped green onions
1/4 lb. spinach leaves, shredded
1/2 lb. Chinese cabbage, shredded
2 tablespoons chopped coriander
1/3 cup dry ramen noodles

Hotpot Dipping Sauce:
6 tablespoons soy sauce
3 tablespoons creamy peanut butter
2 tablespoons rice wine or dry sherry
Dash chili powder
3 tablespoons hot water

Slice lamb thinly and arrange on two large plates. Place broth in a medium-size saucepan with ginger and garlic; simmer 15 minutes. Put green onions, spinach, Chinese cabbage, coriander and noodles in separate serving bowls.

Combine all ingredients for Hotpot Dipping Sauce in a small bowl then divide into 6 small dishes.

Pour broth into fondue pot, add green onions and bring to a boil. Transfer fondue pot to the burner at the table. Each person uses a fondue fork, but preferably a Chinese wire strainer, to hold pieces of food in the broth until cooked. The cooked food is dipped in the sauce before eating. Any remaining spinach and Chinese cabbage can be added to the pot at the end with the coriander and noodles. When the noodles are tender the resulting soup is served in bowls. Makes about 6 servings.

Serve Ginger Sauce, page 59, also.

Savory Roll-Ups

1/4 cup butter
2 shallots, finely chopped
9 slices (6 oz.) lean bacon, chopped
1 lb. chicken livers, trimmed and chopped
1/2 lb. mushrooms, chopped
1/2 cup chicken broth
2 egg yolks
Pinch Italian seasoning
Salt and pepper
3 to 4 sheets filo pastry
1 egg white, slightly beaten

Melt butter in a large frying pan, add shallots and cook 2 minutes. Add bacon; cook 3 to 4 minutes. Stir in chicken livers; cook 3 minutes. Then add mushrooms; cook 3 minutes. Add broth; simmer until almost evaporated. Cool slightly then stir in egg yolks. Add Italian seasoning, salt and pepper. Roughly chop mixture in a blender or food processor; cool.

Cut pastry sheets in 6-inch squares. Place one tablespoon of chicken liver mixture at one end of each square. Fold over each side then roll up the pastry so that it resembles a spring roll. Seal the edges with beaten egg white, then set aside until ready to cook. The roll-ups are deep-fried in hot oil in the fondue pot. Use Chinese wire strainers to immerse and retrieve the roll-ups. Makes about 6 servings.

Chicken Goujons

1-1/2 lbs. chicken breasts, skinned, boned
1/4 cup all-purpose flour
Salt and pepper
3 eggs, lightly beaten
3/4 cup dry bread crumbs

Red-Pepper Sauce:
2 tablespoons butter
1 small onion, chopped
2 red bell peppers, chopped
1 garlic clove, crushed
1 cup chicken broth
Salt and pepper

Cut chicken in long strips about 1/2 inch wide. Mix flour, salt and pepper together. Dust chicken with seasoned flour, dip in beaten egg then coat with bread crumbs. Place in refrigerator to chill.

To make Red-Pepper Sauce, melt butter in a small saucepan. Add onion and cook until soft. Add red bell peppers and garlic and continue to cook over medium heat 5 minutes. Pour in broth and simmer 10 minutes or until peppers are tender.

Pour Red-Pepper Sauce through a sieve into a second saucepan. Season with salt and pepper and reheat. Serve sauce, garnished with a sprig of dill, with the Chicken Goujons which are deep-fried in hot oil in the fondue pot. Makes about 6 servings.

Crunchy Camembert

12 (1-oz.) portions Camembert cheese
2 eggs, lightly beaten
1 cup dry bread crumbs

Blueberry Sauce:
2 teaspoons cornstarch
1/3 cup water
8 oz. blueberries, thawed if frozen
1/4 cup sugar
Dash nutmeg
2 teaspoons lemon juice

Freeze portions of Camembert cheese 1 hour. Dip each cheese portion in beaten egg, then in bread crumbs; repeat and dip again in egg and bread crumbs. Put on a serving plate and chill until needed.

To make Blueberry Sauce, blend cornstarch with water in a medium-size saucepan. Add remaining ingredients and simmer until liquid thickens. Serve warm garnished with a sprig of mint.

The Camembert portions are deep fried in hot oil in the fondue pot. Use Chinese wire strainers, if available, to lift them out of the pot as a fondue fork will pierce the crust and cause the cheese to ooze out. Makes about 6 servings.

Hot Cranberry Dip

1-1/2 cups sugar
2 cups water
1 lb. fresh cranberries
2 tablespoons port

To Serve:
2 lbs. cooked chicken or turkey, diced

In a large saucepan combine sugar with water. Heat to dissolve sugar, then boil 5 minutes.

Add cranberries and simmer about 10 minutes or until skins burst.

Remove saucepan from heat; stir in port. Pour into fondue pot and serve with diced chicken or turkey. Makes about 6 servings.

Meatballs Provençal

1-1/2 lbs. ground beef
1 small onion, finely chopped
2 oz. stuffed olives, finely chopped
1 small egg, beaten
All-purpose flour to coat

Provençal Dip:
1 medium-size eggplant, diced
3 tablespoons olive oil
1 shallot, finely chopped
1 garlic clove, crushed
1 lb. tomatoes, skinned, chopped
1 tablespoon tomato paste
1 tablespoon chopped parsley

Place eggplant in colander; sprinkle with salt and let stand 30 minutes to drain. Mix ingredients for meatballs, season with salt and pepper. With wet hands, roll mixture into 36 small balls then coat in flour. Chill in refrigerator until needed.

To make Provençal Dip, rinse and pat eggplant dry. Heat olive oil in a large saucepan and cook shallot and garlic 2 minutes. Add eggplant and cook over medium heat 10 minutes or until soft. Add tomatoes and tomato paste and continue to cook, covered, 5 to 8 minutes or until tomatoes are reduced almost to a pulp. Stir in parsley. Serve warm with meatballs which are deep-fried in hot oil in the fondue pot. Makes about 6 servings.

Chow Mein Salad

4 oz. Chinese egg noodles
1/4 lb. Chinese pea pods, trimmed
6 oz. bean sprouts, roots trimmed
6 green onions, chopped
1 red bell pepper, finely sliced
1/4 lb. mushrooms, sliced
1 small head leaf lettuce, shredded

Dressing:
1/4 cup sunflower oil
2 tablespoons lemon juice
1 tablespoon soy sauce·
1 (1-inch) piece ginger root, cut in very thin
   strips

2 tablespoons sesame seed

Bring a medium-size saucepan of salted water to
a boil, break up egg noodles and plunge them
into the water. Boil 5 to 6 minutes or until
tender. Drain and allow noodles to cool.

Split pea pods in half and place in a medium-size
bowl. Pour boiling water over the pea pods and
let stand 2 minutes; drain and cool. Put noodles
and pea pods into a salad bowl with remaining
salad ingredients.

Mix together all ingredients for dressing, pour
over salad and toss together. Sprinkle with
sesame seed. Makes 6 to 8 servings.

Summer Vegetable Salad

3/4 lb. eggplant, diced
3 tablespoons olive oil
1 medium-size yellow onion, sliced
3/4 lb. zucchini, sliced
1 red bell pepper, cut in chunks
1 green bell pepper, cut in chunks
1 yellow bell pepper, cut in chunks
3 tomatoes, skinned, chopped
1 tablespoon chopped fresh basil
Salt and pepper
1 tablespoon chopped fresh parsley (optional)

Put eggplant in a colander, sprinkle with salt and let stand 30 minutes to drain. Rinse and dry.

Heat oil in a large skillet, add eggplant and onion and cook over medium heat 5 minutes. Add zucchini and peppers and cook over low heat 15 minutes, turning them over until tender.

Transfer vegetables to a large serving bowl. Stir in tomatoes, basil, salt and pepper; let cool. Chill before serving. Sprinkle with chopped parsley. Makes 6 to 8 servings.

Potato Salad

1-1/2 lbs. new potatoes, scrubbed
6 green onions, chopped
1 tablespoon chopped fresh parsley
1 teaspoon chopped fresh marjoram
1 tablespoon chopped fresh dill

Yogurt Dressing:
5 tablespoons plain low-fat yogurt
3 tablespoons mayonnaise
2 teaspoons lemon juice
1 teaspoon Dijon mustard
Salt and pepper

Cook potatoes in boiling salted water until tender; drain and allow to cool. Cut potatoes in thick slices and put in a serving bowl. Reserve some chopped green onions and herbs for garnishing then add remainder to potatoes; toss together.

Blend together all ingredients for Yogurt Dressing and pour over potatoes; chill. Mix lightly, garnish with reserved green onions and herbs and serve. Makes about 6 servings.

Mixed Leaf Salad

1/2 head romaine lettuce, shredded
1/2 head iceberg lettuce, shredded
1 medium-size avocado
2 teaspoons lemon juice
1 green bell pepper, sliced
1/2 cucumber, sliced
6 green onions, chopped
Watercress, trimmed
Curly endive
3 celery stalks, chopped

Dressing:
2 tablespoons walnut oil
2 tablespoons sunflower oil
1 tablespoon white-wine vinegar
1/2 teaspoon Dijon mustard
Salt and pepper

Put lettuce in a large salad bowl. Cut avocado in half, remove seed and peel. Cut in slices and coat with lemon juice. Add avocado slices and remaining salad ingredients to lettuce in bowl.

Mix all ingredients for dressing together, pour over salad and toss together. Makes about 6 to 8 servings.

Caribbean Coleslaw

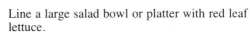

1 head red leaf lettuce
1/2 head iceberg lettuce, shredded
5 celery stalks, finely sliced
2 medium-size carrots, grated
1/2 small pineapple, cut in chunks
3 oz. fresh dates, pitted, chopped
2 oz. pecans or walnuts, chopped

Dressing:
3 tablespoons mayonnaise
Grated peel and juice of 1 lime
2 tablespoons sunflower oil
Salt and pepper

Line a large salad bowl or platter with red leaf lettuce.

In a separate bowl put all other salad ingredients except pecans; mix together. Blend all ingredients for dressing, pour over the salad and toss.

Spoon salad into prepared bowl and sprinkle with pecans. Makes about 6 servings.

Rice & Spinach Salad

2-1/2 cups long grain rice
2 tablespoons oil
1 bunch green onions, chopped
1 (10-oz.) pkg. frozen chopped spinach, thawed
   and well drained
Salt and pepper

In a medium-size saucepan bring 4 cups salted water to a boil. Keep the water simmering while adding the rice; cover and cook 15 minutes until rice is soft and water is absorbed.

In a large skillet, heat oil and cook green onions 3 to 4 minutes; stir into rice.

Add spinach, salt and pepper to rice. Stir together and heat through 1 to 2 minutes. Serve warm garnished with a slice of lemon. Alternatively, allow rice to cool before serving. Makes about 6 servings.

Galliano & Grapefruit Dip

2 large grapefruit
2 tablespoons sugar
2 tablespoons Galliano
1 tablespoon cornstarch
2 tablespoons whipping cream

To Serve:
1 medium-size crenshaw, Santa Claus or honey-dew melon

Cut melon in half and remove seeds. Using a melon baller, cut out as many balls as possible.

Grate enough peel from the grapefruit to yield 1 teaspoon, then squeeze the juice from both grapefruit. Place sugar, Galliano and cornstarch in a small saucepan and blend together. Stir in grapefruit juice and peel, then heat until boiling; simmer 1 minute.

Remove from heat and stir in whipping cream. Pour into a serving bowl, garnish with a sprig of mint and serve warm with melon balls. Makes about 6 servings.

Frothy Champagne Dip

3 eggs
1/4 cup sugar
1 tablespoon finely grated orange peel
2/3 cup whipping cream
2/3 cup medium dry champagne

To Serve:
fresh strawberries and cubes of Quick Almond Cake, page 69

Put eggs, sugar and orange peel in a small bowl. Set bowl over a pan of simmering water and beat until mixture is thick and fluffy.

Remove bowl from heat and beat in whipping cream and champagne.

Pour sauce into a warmed bowl and serve with strawberries and cubes of cake. Makes about 6 servings.

Hot Caramel Sauce

1 cup whipping cream
1/3 cup butter
1/3 cup packed brown sugar

To Serve:
vanilla and chocolate ice cream; 4 oz. chopped almonds, lightly toasted

At least 2 hours before serving the meal, prepare the ice cream. Soften ice cream slightly. Using an ice-cream scoop, make small vanilla and small chocolate scoops. Place them on a baking tray, coat with almonds and quickly return to the freezer.

To make Hot Caramel Sauce, heat whipping cream and butter, stirring constantly, in a heavy saucepan until butter melts.

Add brown sugar; continue to stir until dissolved and the mixture comes to a boil. Boil 2 minutes or until thick and glossy. Serve with prepared ice cream. Makes about 6 servings.

Drambuie Cream Fondue

4 teaspoons cornstarch
1-1/4 cups whipping cream
1 tablespoon sugar
3 tablespoons Drambuie

Lemon Cake:
2 eggs
1/2 cup margarine, softened
1/2 cup sugar
1 cup self-rising flour
Dash baking powder
Grated peel and juice of 1/2 lemon

To Serve:
3 medium-size oranges, segmented

Preheat oven to 350F (175C). Grease one 7-inch-square cake pan. Put all ingredients for Lemon Cake in a medium-size bowl and beat together 3 minutes.

Pour batter into prepared pan and bake 25 minutes or until golden and firm to the touch. Cool on a wire rack; cut in small squares.

To make Drambuie Cream Fondue, blend cornstarch with whipping cream in a small saucepan. Cook over medium heat until thick and smooth. Stir in sugar and Drambuie then pour into a serving dish. Arrange segments of orange and squares of cake around the dish. Garnish fondue with thin strips of orange peel. Makes about 6 servings.

Beignets

1/4 cup butter
1-1/4 cups water
1-1/2 cups all-purpose flour, sifted
3 large eggs, beaten
1/2 teaspoon vanilla extract
5 teaspoons sugar

Orange Sauce:
4 large oranges
2 medium-size lemons
4 teaspoons arrowroot
2/3 cup water
1 tablespoon butter
1/3 cup sugar

To make Orange Sauce, grate the peel from 2 oranges and 1 lemon.

Squeeze the juice from all of the oranges and lemons. In a small saucepan, blend arrowroot with a portion of the fruit juice. Add remaining juice and water and bring to a boil; simmer 1 minute. Stir in orange and lemon peels, butter and sugar; simmer 2 minutes.

To make Beignets, put butter in a medium-size saucepan with water and bring to a boil. Remove pan from heat and add flour; beat to make a smooth paste. Gradually beat in eggs, vanilla extract and 5 teaspoons sugar. Heat oil or shortening in a deep-fat fryer to 350F (175C). Drop teaspoonfuls of the batter into the oil, cooking only a few Beignets at a time. Cook 6 to 8 minutes or until golden brown. Remove with a slotted spoon, drain on paper towels and dust with sugar. Keep cooked Beignets warm until ready to serve. Pour Orange Sauce into fondue pot, place over burner at the table and serve with hot Beignets. Makes about 6 servings.

Creamy Kiwi Dip

3 kiwi fruit, peeled
12 oz. cream cheese blended with 3 tablespoons
  milk
1 tablespoon sugar

Melting Moments:
1/2 cup butter
1/3 cup sugar
1 egg yolk
A few drops vanilla extract
1-1/4 cups self-rising flour
1 cup crushed cornflakes

To make Melting Moments, cream butter and sugar together until light and fluffy. Beat in egg yolk and extract. Gradually blend in flour to make a stiff dough. Chill 15 minutes.

Preheat oven to 375F (190C). Grease two baking sheets. Shape dough into 30 small balls and lightly press each into crushed cornflakes. Place 1 inch apart on prepared baking sheets and bake 15 minutes or until golden brown. Cool on wire racks.

To make Creamy Kiwi Dip, put peeled kiwi fruit in a bowl and mash with a fork. Stir in cream cheese mixture and sugar; mix well. Spoon dip into a serving bowl and serve with Melting Moments. Makes about 6 servings.

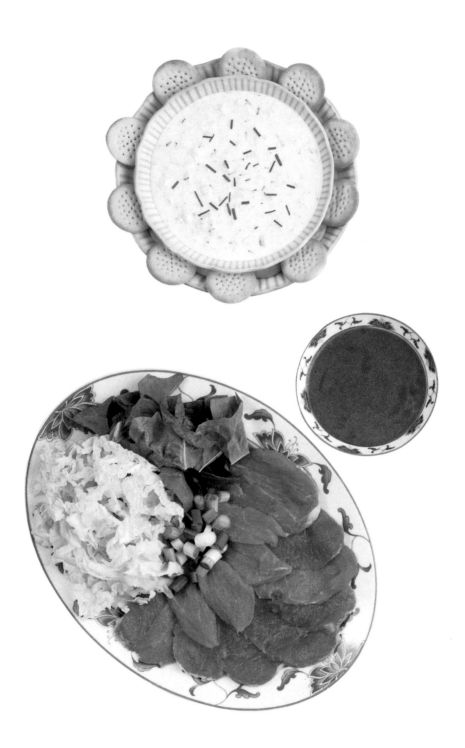

—————————— MENU ONE——————————
Shrimp Dip, page 84;
Mongolian Hotpot, page 90;
Chow Mcin Salad, page 96;
Galliano & Grapefruit Dip, page 102.

——— **MENU TWO** ———
Aioli, page 85;
Savory Roll-Ups, page 91;
Summer Vegetable Salad, page 97;
Frothy Champagne Dip, page 103.

MENU THREE

Guacamole, page 86;
Chicken Goujons, page 92;
Potato Salad, page 98;
Hot Caramel Sauce, page 104.

MENU FOUR

Tapenade Dip, page 87;
Crunchy Camembert, page 93;
Mixed Leaf Salad, page 99;
Drambuie Cream Fondue, page 105.

—————— MENU FIVE ——————
Bagna Cauda, page 88;
Hot Cranberry Dip, page 94;
Caribbean Coleslaw, page 100;
Beignets, page 106.

MENU SIX

Crab & Cheese Dip, page 89;
Meatballs Provençal, page 95;
Rice & Spinach Salad, page 101;
Creamy Kiwi Dip, page 107.

INDEX